D1116193

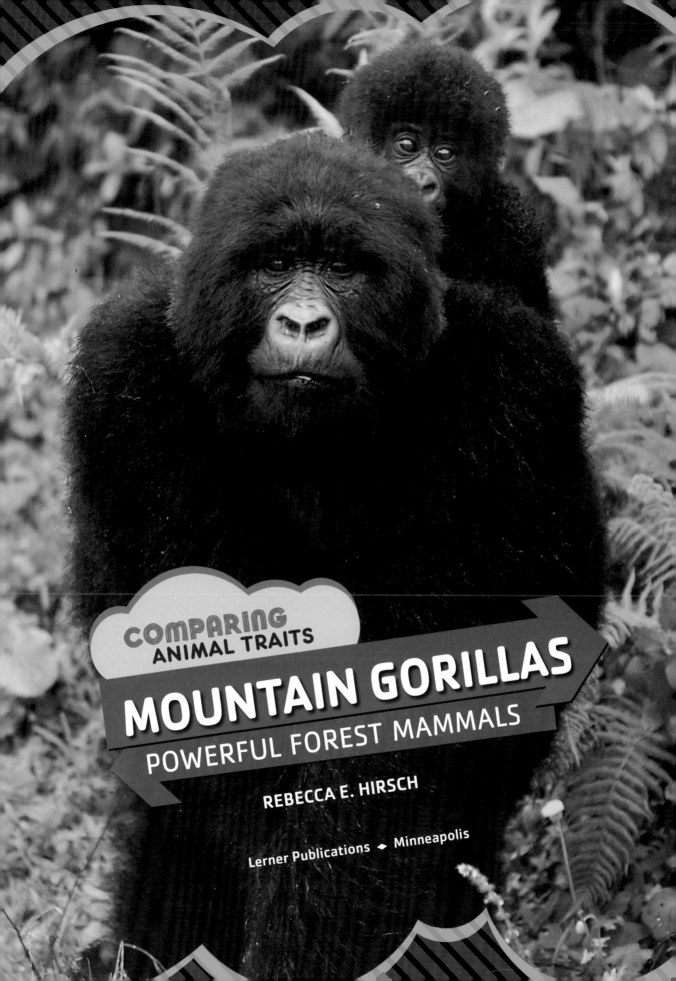

COMPARING ANIMAL TRAITS

MOUNTAIN GORILLAS
POWERFUL FOREST MAMMALS

REBECCA E. HIRSCH

Lerner Publications ◆ Minneapolis

Lerner Publications Company
A division of Lerner Publishing Group, Inc.
241 First Avenue North
Minneapolis, MN 55401 USA

For reading levels and more information, look up this title at www.lernerbooks.com.

Photo Acknowledgments

The images in this book are used with the permission of: Ralph H. Bendjebar/Danita Delimont Photography/Newscom, p. 1; © Mary Ann McDonald/Visuals Unlimited, Inc., p. 4; © EBFoto/Shutterstock.com, p. 5; © Steve Bloom Images/SuperStock, pp. 6, 9 (left); © Kate Duffell/Dreamstime.com, p. 7; © Barman1965/Dreamstime.com, p. 8 (left); Joe McDonald/NHPA/Photoshot/Newscom, p. 8 (right); © iStockphoto.com/ChrisCrafter, p. 9 (right); Mint Images-Frans Lanting Mint Images/Newscom, p. 10; © Jum Jarvis/Visuals Unlimited, Inc., p. 11 (left); © John Warburton Lee/SuperStock, p. 11 (right); © Mapping Specialists, Ltd., Madison, WI, p. 12; © The Africa Image Library/Alamy, p. 13 (top); © Joe McDonald/CORBIS, p. 13 (bottom); © Ammit Jack/Shutterstock.com, p. 14; © Minden Pictures/SuperStock, pp. 15 (left), 17 (right), 21(left), 25 (bottom), 29 (right); Joe & Mary Ann McDonald/Danita Delimont Photography/Newscom, p. 15 (right); Jurgen & Christine Sohns/FLPA imageBROKER/Newscom, p. 16; © Pal Teravagimov/Shutterstock.com, p. 17 (left); © Mark Cooney/Dreamstime.com, p. 18; © akg-images /Newscom, p. 19 (top); © NaturePL/SuperStock, p. 19; © iStockphoto.com/TobiasBischof, p. 20; © iStockphoto.com/Maxlevoyou, p. 21 (right); © Rinus Baak/Dreamstime.com, p. 22; © Lightwave Photography, Inc./Animals Animals, p. 23; © James Hager/Robert Harding Picture Library/SuperStock, p. 24; © Suzi Eszterhas/Minden Pictures/Getty Images, p. 25 (top); © age fotostock/SuperStock, p. 26; © NHPA/SuperStock, p. 27 (bottom); ©500px.com/brandonoverland, p. 27; © Robert Maier/Animals Animals, p. 28; © NHPA/SuperStock, p. 29 (left).

Front cover: Vincent Gesser/NHPA/Photoshot/Newscom.
Back cover: © Joe McDonald/Shutterstock.com.

Main body text set in Calvert MT Std 12/18. Typeface provided by Monotype Typography.

Library of Congress Cataloging-in-Publication Data

Hirsch, Rebecca E., author.
    Mountain gorillas : powerful forest mammals / by Rebecca E. Hirsch.
      pages   cm. — (Comparing animal traits)
    Summary: "This book covers information (life cycle, appearance, habitat) about the mountain gorilla. Each chapter discusses an aspect of the mountain gorilla's life, comparing the gorilla to a similar mammal and to a very different mammal."—Provided by publisher.
    Includes index.
    ISBN: 978–1–4677–5580–1 (lib. bdg. : alk. paper)
    ISBN: 978–1–4677–6219–9 (EB pdf)
    1. Mountain gorilla—Behavior—Juvenile literature. 2. Mountain gorilla—Juvenile literature.
    I. Title.
    QL737.P94H57 2015
    599.884—dc23   2014018811

Manufactured in the United States of America
1 — BP —12/31/14

TABLE OF CONTENTS

Introduction
LET'S MEET MOUNTAIN GORILLAS 4

Chapter 1
WHAT DO MOUNTAIN GORILLAS LOOK LIKE? 6

Chapter 2
WHERE MOUNTAIN GORILLAS LIVE 12

Chapter 3
LIFE IN THE GORILLA TROOP 18

CHAPTER 4
THE LIFE CYCLE OF MOUNTAIN GORILLAS 24

Mountain Gorilla Trait Chart   30
Glossary   31
Selected Bibliography   32
Further Information   32
Index   32

LET'S MEET MOUNTAIN GORILLAS

A family of mountain gorillas rests in a clearing. As the adults doze on the ground, the young gorillas chase one another. They wrestle and tumble, testing their strength. Mountain gorillas are mammals, a kind of animal. Other kinds of animals include insects, fish, amphibians, reptiles, and birds.

Young mountain gorillas love to roll around and play.

Mountain gorillas have fur and are warm-blooded.

All mammals share certain traits. They are all vertebrates, animals with backbones. They are warm-blooded, which means their bodies stay warm even when it's cold outside. They usually give birth to live young, although a few mammals lay eggs. They all have hair or fur. All female mammals make milk for their babies.

Mountain gorillas have these and other traits in common with other mammals. Yet they also have traits that set them apart. Mountain gorillas are powerful, plant-eating mammals. You can find them in the forests of Africa.

CHAPTER 1

WHAT DO MOUNTAIN GORILLAS LOOK LIKE?

Mountain gorillas are the largest of the great apes. This family of mammals also includes humans, bonobos, chimpanzees, and orangutans. A male mountain gorilla stands as tall as a grown human but weighs about twice as much. Female mountain gorillas are smaller than the males.

The face of a mountain gorilla has a browridge above the eyes, a flat nose, and flaring nostrils. Shaggy dark hair covers most of a mountain gorilla's body. Its face, feet, chest, palms, and the soles of its feet are bare. As a male grows older, a patch of hair on his back turns silvery gray. He is then known as a silverback.

DID YOU KNOW?

Full-grown male mountain gorillas may stand nearly **6 FEET** (1.8 meters) tall and weigh 400 pounds (181 kilograms) or more.

The mountain gorilla's large hands have four thick fingers and a thumb. Its front arms are longer than its legs. Mountain gorillas travel by walking on all fours. They curl their fingers and walk on their knuckles. They also climb trees with their strong limbs. Younger, lighter gorillas are better climbers than older gorillas.

An adult male mountain gorilla is known as a silverback.

MOUNTAIN GORILLAS VS. CHIMPANZEES

Chimpanzees climb in the trees of a forest. One young chimp slides down a trunk and joins other chimpanzees on the ground. Chimpanzees are another member of the great ape family. Mountain gorillas and chimpanzees look a lot alike, although chimpanzees are smaller. A male chimpanzee is about half the size of a male gorilla.

Both mountain gorillas and chimpanzees have large browridges, smooth skin, and black fur. Young chimpanzees are born with pale faces, but their skin darkens as the animals age. As with male mountain gorillas, the coats of male and female adult chimpanzees can turn silver on the back.

A mountain gorilla (*left*) and a chimpanzee (*right*) are both members of the great ape family.

COMPARE IT!

MOUNTAIN GORILLAS VS. **CHIMPANZEES**

5 TO 6 FEET
(1.5 TO 1.8 M)
◀ HEIGHT ▶
4 TO 5.5 FEET
(1.2 TO 1.7 M)

300 TO 485 POUNDS
(135 TO 220 KG)
◀ WEIGHT ▶
70 TO 130 POUNDS
(32 TO 60 KG)

Both animals have long, powerful arms and hands with four fingers and a thumb. Chimpanzees are better climbers than mountain gorillas. Their lighter bodies make climbing less difficult. But both mountain gorillas and chimpanzees travel by knuckle-walking while on the ground.

MOUNTAIN GORILLAS VS. NAKED MOLE RATS

Naked mole rats inhabit burrows in East Africa. They live together in colonies and spend their entire lives underground. These mammals are much smaller than mountain gorillas. You could hold several naked mole rats in one hand.

The body of a naked mole rat is built for underground travel.

Unlike a mountain gorilla (*left*), a naked mole rat (*right*) uses its teeth to dig as well as to eat.

Naked mole rats look very different from mountain gorillas. They are adapted for living underground. Their sausage-shaped bodies and short, powerful legs help them move through tight tunnels. Their big teeth and snouts let them dig through dirt. The eyes of naked mole rats are tiny and weak. But mole rats can use their eyes to sense air currents within dark burrows.

Like all mammals, naked mole rats have hair. But the hair isn't thick and dark like that of a mountain gorilla. The naked mole rat has only a few hairs on its body. Being nearly hairless may help naked mole rats stay cool in the tunnels. Mole rats also have sensitive hairs on their snouts. The hairs help the animal feel its way in the tunnels.

CHAPTER 2

WHERE MOUNTAIN GORILLAS LIVE

Mountain gorillas inhabit the forest-covered mountains of central Africa. These areas are known as cloud forests. Weather in cloud forests is cool and misty. A layer of clouds bathes the treetops.

Mountain gorillas move through their habitat by knuckle-walking. They travel to open, sunny areas of the forest to feed. They rest in nests of branches or leaves. They build these nests on the ground or in trees. During the day, the gorillas forage for leaves and branches in different parts of the forest. They put new nests together each night.

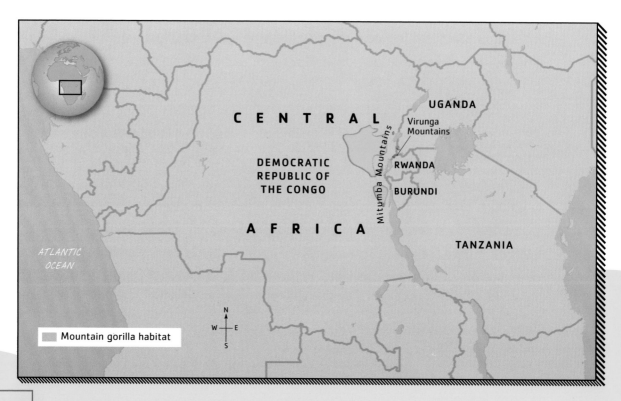

CENTRAL

UGANDA

Virunga
Mountains

DEMOCRATIC
REPUBLIC OF
THE CONGO

RWANDA

BURUNDI

Mitumba Mountains

AFRICA

TANZANIA

ATLANTIC
OCEAN

N
W — E
S

Mountain gorilla habitat

An African cloud forest is full of the plant life that mountain gorillas need to survive.

Humans sometimes invade mountain gorilla habitats. People have chopped down cloud forests for fuel, farmland, and housing. They have fought wars in these areas. Hunters have also killed gorillas. For these reasons, mountain gorillas are in danger of extinction. In 2013, only about 880 mountain gorillas remained in the world. But with the help of scientists, park rangers, and other concerned people in central Africa, the population is slowly growing.

DID YOU KNOW?
A 400-pound (181 kg) gorilla can eat **40 POUNDS** (18 kg) of leaves, stems, and shoots each day.

MOUNTAIN GORILLAS VS. SPECTACLED BEARS

Spectacled bears live in the Andes Mountains of South America. This bear's mountain habitats are similar to those of the mountain gorilla. Both mammals live in cloud forests. Like mountain gorillas, spectacled bears mainly eat plants.

Spectacled bears like fruit, cacti, and berries. They are good climbers and can forage for food in the trees of cloud forests. They will also eat insects, birds, and small mammals. They sometimes raid cornfields or kill farm animals.

Spectacled bears occupy cloud forests within South America.

Both mountain gorillas (*left*) and the spectacled bear (*right*) build nests in which to sleep.

Like mountain gorillas, spectacled bears build nests. They make these nests in trees, using broken branches. Spectacled bears use their nests as platforms for feeding. Like mountain gorillas, they also can sleep in their nests.

Both mountain gorilla and spectacled bear populations are in danger. Hunters and farmers in South America have killed many bears. People have destroyed their forests. The number of living spectacled bears has fallen.

MOUNTAIN GORILLAS VS. RACCOONS

Raccoons forage for food throughout North and Central America. The habitats of raccoons are different from the habitat of mountain gorillas. Mountain gorillas live only in cloud forests, but raccoons live in many places. They inhabit forests, marshes, grasslands, and cities, as long as water is near.

Unlike mountain gorillas, which eat mostly plants, raccoons will eat almost anything. These mammals snack on plants and smaller animals. They raid farm fields and take food from garbage cans. They will even beg beside a road if they know passersby will give them food.

Many raccoons find shelter inside trees.

Mountain gorillas sleep in nests, but raccoons sleep in dens. A raccoon den might be in a high tree, a fallen log, or a rock crevice. Raccoons even build dens in attics sometimes. Unlike mountain gorillas, raccoons have thrived while living near people.

COMPARE IT!

MOUNTAIN GORILLAS VS. **RACCOONS**

	HABITAT	
CLOUD FORESTS		FORESTS, MARSHES, GRASSLANDS, FARMS, CITIES

	GEOGRAPHIC RANGE	
MOUNTAINS OF CENTRAL ASIA		NORTH AND CENTRAL AMERICA

	MAIN FOOD	
Plant leaves and stems		Frogs, fish, mice, insects, bird eggs, nuts, seeds, fruit, crops, garbage

CHAPTER 3

LIFE IN THE GORILLA TROOP

Mountain gorillas live in family groups called troops. A silverback male, a few younger males (called blackbacks), several females, and their young make up a troop. The silverback is the head of the family. He decides where the troop will eat. He gives a sign before the troop moves to feed in another part of the forest. He keeps everyone in the family in order.

The members of a gorilla troop usually follow the signals of one powerful leader.

DID YOU KNOW?
The gigantic gorilla in the movie *King Kong* is a scary **BEAST**. But real gorillas are calm unless threatened. Most mountain gorillas would rather eat or rest than fight.

Sometimes a blackback challenges the silverback or threatens the troop. In response, the silverback will hoot and beat his chest with cupped hands. He may throw things or let out a huge roar. But troop life is usually peaceful.

Mountain gorillas eat together in the morning. At midday, they rest together. The young tumble on the ground and play. In the afternoon, the gorillas resume eating. At night, they build nests and settle in to sleep.

Mountain gorillas sometimes communicate by pounding their chests.

MOUNTAIN GORILLAS VS. HIPPOPOTAMUSES

Hippopotamuses inhabit lakes, swamps, and rivers in Africa. Hippos and mountain gorillas have similar behaviors. Both of these mammals live in groups. A grown male leader, females, and their young make up a herd of hippos. Younger males tend to live together in their own groups.

Like mountain gorillas, hippos have a daily routine. During the day, hippos keep cool by dozing in the water. At sunset, they move to land. They feed on grass during the night. A herd of hippos, like a gorilla troop, sleeps together.

A younger male hippo may sometimes challenge the male leader in his herd. This is similar to mountain gorilla behavior. The male hippos will stand with their mouths open wide and show their long teeth. They are testing who is bigger and stronger. Often the smaller hippo will back down. If he doesn't, the two may fight.

Two hippos test their strength.

COMPARE IT!

MOUNTAIN GORILLAS

VS.

HIPPOS

TROOP ◀ NAME OF GROUP ▶ **SCHOOL OR HERD**

2 TO 30 ◀ TYPICAL SIZE OF GROUP ▶ **10 TO 30**

SILVERBACK MALE ◀ LEADER OF GROUP ▶ **LARGE MALE**

MOUNTAIN GORILLAS VS. MOUNTAIN LIONS

Mountain lions live in North and South America. They are also called cougars or pumas. Unlike gorillas, mountain lions are predators. Along with their different diets, these mammals have different behaviors.

Mountain lions usually live by themselves.

DID YOU KNOW?
Unlike mountain gorillas, mountain lions can sometimes be dangerous to people. **ATTACKS** are rare, though. Most mountain lions avoid people.

Mountain lions do not live in groups. These mammals live and hunt alone. But they do send messages to one another. Mountain lions mark their territories with urine and by scratching on trees. They growl and hiss. These messages warn other mountain lions away from their territories.

Mountain gorillas have a set routine, but mountain lions do not. Some mountain lions hunt at sunrise and sunset. Others hunt at night. Mountain lions eat deer, pigs, beavers, and raccoons. Sometimes prey is plentiful. A mountain lion might hide extra food and rest while it eats the stored prey. Sometimes food is hard to find. Then a mountain lion will travel far to search for prey.

CHAPTER 4

THE LIFE CYCLE OF MOUNTAIN GORILLAS

A 400-pound (181 kg) adult mountain gorilla starts life as a tiny, helpless infant. Newborn gorillas weigh only 4 to 5 pounds (1.8 to 2.3 kg). As with nearly all female mammals, mountain gorilla mothers give birth to live young. Each female gives birth to one baby at a time.

A mother gorilla feeds milk to her baby. The baby mountain gorilla clings to the mother's belly as she moves through the forest. At two months, the youngster is crawling. At four months, it can ride on its mother's back. The mother nurses and carries the young gorilla for about four years. During this period, the silverback in the troop plays with and helps protect the young.

Mountain gorilla mothers give their babies milk until the babies can eat solid food.

DID YOU KNOW?
YOUNG gorillas love to chase one another through the trees and play follow-the-leader.

Mountain gorillas are mature in ten to fifteen years. At that time, both males and females leave to join or start another troop. These gorillas have inherited traits from their parents, such as long arms for knuckle-walking and a social nature. These traits will help them survive in the mountain forests, where they may live to be forty to fifty years old.

A young gorilla rides on the back of its mother.

Meerkats live in the deserts and dry grasslands of southern Africa. Despite the animal's name, it is not a cat but a member of the mongoose family. Mountain gorillas and meerkats both live in family groups. They share similar life cycles.

Meerkat mothers give birth to between two and four pups at a time.

DID YOU KNOW?
When meerkats forage, a few family members **STAND GUARD.** If a guard spots a hawk or an eagle, the guard gives a shrill call. The meerkats run for cover.

Like mountain gorillas and nearly all mammals, female meerkats give birth to live young. Meerkat mothers have two to four babies at a time. Meerkat babies are tiny. The pups snuggle close to their mother inside their den. When they are four months old, around the age when mountain gorillas begin to crawl, meerkat pups start to venture out on their own.

Similar to mountain gorilla fathers, meerkat fathers help raise the young. Meerkat fathers play with the pups. They teach them how to forage for insects, small animals, fruit, and eggs. They also help guard the young from predators. Meerkats that outwit predators may live for fifteen years.

Like young mountain gorillas, young meerkats love to play.

MOUNTAIN GORILLAS VS. HAMSTERS

Hamsters inhabit grasslands, farm fields, and riverbanks.
These mammals are native to Europe and Asia. People in the
United States may know them as pets. Hamsters have very
different life cycles than mountain gorillas.

Hamster families live in dens. Inside the den, a hamster female
gives birth to live young. A single hamster litter includes four to
twelve young. Unlike male mountain gorillas, fathers in hamster
families don't help raise their young. The mother provides all the
care. Female hamsters nurse their young and stay with them.

Young hamsters mature more quickly than young mountain
gorillas. By three weeks, hamsters have stopped nursing. At
two months, young hamsters are ready to live on their own.
Mountain gorillas are just starting to crawl at this age. Hamsters
also live much shorter lives than mountain gorillas. Hamsters may
live up to four years, but mountain gorillas may live for forty years
or even longer.

Young hamsters nurse for the
first three weeks of their lives.

28

COMPARE IT!

MOUNTAIN GORILLAS

VS.

HAMSTERS

MOUNTAIN GORILLAS		HAMSTERS
LESS THAN 1	NUMBER OF OFFSPRING IN ONE YEAR	8 TO 24
10 TO 15 YEARS	TYPICAL AGE AT MATURITY	2 MONTHS
40 TO 50 YEARS	LIFE SPAN	2 TO 4 YEARS

MOUNTAIN GORILLA TRAIT CHART

This book explored mountain gorillas and the ways they are similar to and different from other mammals. What other mammals would you like to learn about?

	WARM-BLOODED	HAIR ON BODY	GIVES BIRTH TO LIVE YOUNG	LONG FRONT ARMS	AT RISK OF EXTINCTION	LIVES IN GROUPS
MOUNTAIN GORILLAS	X	X	X	X	X	X
CHIMPANZEE	X	X	X	X	X	X
NAKED MOLE RAT	X	X	X			X
SPECTACLED BEAR	X	X	X	X	X	
RACCOON	X	X	X			
HIPPOPOTAMUS	X	X	X		X	X
MOUNTAIN LION	X	X	X			
MEERKAT	X	X	X			X
HAMSTER	X	X	X			

GLOSSARY

adapted: suited to living in a particular environment

extinction: the state of no longer existing

forage: to search an area for food

habitat: an environment where an animal naturally lives. A habitat is the area where an animal can find food, water, air, shelter, and a place to raise its young.

mature: having reached adulthood

population: all the members of one type of animal

predators: animals that hunt, or prey on, other animals

prey: an animal that is hunted and killed by a predator for food

territories: areas that are occupied and defended by an animal or group of animals

traits: features that are inherited from parents. Body size and fur color are examples of inherited traits.

LERNER

SOURCE

Expand learning beyond the printed book. Download free, complementary educational resources for this book from our website, www.lerneresource.com.

SELECTED BIBLIOGRAPHY

Animal Diversity Web. University of Michigan Museum of Zoology. May 5, 2014. http://animaldiversity.ummz.umich.edu/.

"Animal Facts." Animal Fact Guide. May 8 2014. http://www.animalfactguide.com/animal-facts/.

Gould, Edwin, and George McKay. *The Encyclopedia of Mammals*. Sydney: Academic Press, 1998.

"The Great Apes" Wildlife Conservation Society. May 2, 2014. http://www.wcs.org/saving-wildlife/great-apes.aspx.

IUCN 2013. IUCN Red List of Threatened Species. Version 2013.2. May 9, 2014. http://www.iucnredlist.org.

"Mammals." *National Geographic*. May 5, 2014. http://animals.nationalgeographic.com/animals/mammals/.

"Primate Factsheets." *Primate Info Net*. National Primate Research Center, University of Wisconsin–Madison. May 5, 2014. http://pin.primate.wisc.edu/factsheets/.

FURTHER INFORMATION

African Wildlife Foundation—Gallery http://www.awf.org/wildlife-conservation/all Learn more about animals that live in cloud forests and other places in Africa. Visitors can search by picture to find maps, photos, and video clips.

The Dian Fossey Gorilla Fund International—Creative Kids Help Save Gorillas http://gorillafund.org/kids_save_gorillas Visit this site to read the inspiring stories of kids who are helping to save gorillas.

Family of Mountain Gorillas—*Cousins*—BBC

http://www.youtube.com/watch?v=ODyB9i6bGwQ Watch this video clip from the nature series *Cousins* to see a family of mountain gorillas eating and playing in an African forest.

Wojahn, Rebecca Hogue. *A Cloud Forest Food Chain: A Who-Eats-What Adventure in Africa*. Minneapolis: Lerner Publications, 2010. Learn more about the food chains in an African cloud forest with the help of this book.

INDEX

endangered species, 13, 15

gorilla troops, 18–19

mammal features, 5
mountain gorilla comparisons: vs. chimpanzees, 8–9; vs. hamsters, 28–29; vs. hippopotamuses, 20–21; vs. meerkats, 26–27; vs. mountain lions, 22–23; vs. naked mole rats, 10–11; vs. raccoons, 16–17; vs. spectacled bear, 14–15
mountain gorillas: communication, 18–19; diet, 13, 16–17; habitat, 5, 12–13; life cycle, 24–25; size, 6, 9; traits, 6–7

silverbacks, 6–7, 18–19, 24

trait chart, 30
types of habitats: burrows, 10–11; cities, 16–17; cloud forests, 12–15; deserts, 26; grasslands, 16–17, 26, 28; marshes, 16–17; swamps, 20